Green Surprise of Passion:

Writings of a Trauma Therapist

Green Surprise of Passion:

Writings of a Trauma Therapist

Shirley Glubka

Blade of Grass Press

1998

Grateful acknowledgement is made to those who previously
published parts of *Green Surprise of Passion*.

"As If" was published in *The Republican Journal* of Belfast, Maine
    (May 5, 1994).
"Grief" was published in *Network: Maine Women's Newspaper*,
    Blue Hill, Maine, (August, 1993).
"Mind Split" (a portion of "Once Upon a Time Can Be Reversed")
    was published in "Tinker's Shop," (Elgin, Oregon, Quarterly
    Review of *The Elgin Recorder*, Vol. 3, No. 1, March, 1998).
"To Follow" was published as "Over the Chasm" in *Kennebec:
    Portfolio of Maine Writing* (March, 1992).
"Two" was published in *Out of the Cradle: An Uncommon Reader*
    (Vol. 1, No. 3, Fall, 1995).
"Unfinished" was published in *Lesbians at Midlife: The Creative
    Transition* (San Francisco, Spinster Books, 1991).

––––––––––

"Green Surprise of Passion" appeared first, in quite different form,
as a Masters Thesis titled "Something Pulled at Me." It is available
at the Fogler Library, University of Maine, Orono, Maine.

ISBN 0-9666481-0-2

Printed by Odyssey Press, Inc.
Dover, New Hampshire

Cover design by Shirley Glubka

Published by
Blade of Grass Press
RFD 1, Box 1358
Stockton Springs, Maine 04981
Phone (207) 469-2917

Dedicated to my clients.

Acknowledgments

I am grateful to everyone who encouraged me in this particular project and to all who have nurtured my life with language, starting with my mother and father, Harriet and Addison Glubka, who taught me to value my mind.

Through the decades, friends and writers have been with me, shaping my work. Special among these are: Sonia Gernes, Frances Zarod Rominski, Ellen Goldberg, Carol Erdman, Melanie Kaye/Kantrowitz, Diane Nowicki, Solla Carrock, Jennifer Walker, Amy Kesselman, and Danny Lewis.

In the last twelve years, while I was developing as a trauma therapist, getting my second (midlife) graduate degree—this time in English—and wrestling with the ever-changing manuscript that would become "Green Surprise," many teachers, fellow students, writers and therapists gave generous support. Key among these were: Constance Hunting, Jeri Onitskansky, Karen Saum, Laura Levenson, Lucy Quimby, and Carol Romeo Veits.

My clients have given so much to this project, without knowing it. They have offered challenge, shared the tender places in their lives, and taught me how humor, hope, and courage can balance even the deepest psychological pain, even the worst horror.

Through it all, my life partner, Virginia Holmes, has been at the center, taking me to deeper and more interesting places as a writer, a therapist, and a person.

My thanks to all.

CONTENTS

VI. Prose:
in which the therapist
imagines the mind of the client

VII.Excerpts:
from the therapist's journal.....47

VIII. Poetry:
of owls, mosquitoes,
dragons, and other things

IX. Epilogue

PREFACE

Finding the Form

It was the mid-1980's. My life as a psychotherapist was changing. Clients sat in terror, bombarded with images and sensations, struggling to tell me chaotic, fragmented stories. Or they avoided the stories. There were long periods of tense silence in the therapy room; sudden switches of personality; eruptions of rage; intervals of sardonic humor; strategies, manipulations, defenses; strange games of humankind.

I had begun to see clients who were survivors of severe and prolonged childhood abuse, most of them women. Some of them had experienced sadistic, ritualized abuse, often in a group context, sometimes with satanic content. Some of them had developed multiple personalities as a way of dividing overwhelming experience into (barely) manageable pieces. My training and previous work had done little to prepare me for what I was hearing and seeing.

This collection of writings sprouted from that very particular soil. It could not have come out of any other ground. Before then, and after, my work life was different. Before then, and after, I myself was different.

I was not a new therapist. I was in my forties at the time. Nevertheless, I, like my clients, was overwhelmed. I valued balance as much as I valued anything in life and I tried to keep it. When I couldn't keep my balance, I imagined it, a steady way of being I would not agree to lose. I also valued passion, the stuff that gives life depth. Doing therapy with trauma survivors pulled my deepest passion into usable shape. This was a wonderful, absorbing, stimulating process—and always on the verge of being too much. I thought about my work virtually all of the time. I needed to talk about my work with colleagues in detail and repeatedly. And I wrote. I was like a cow in a strange new field, eating. I took what came to me from my clients and I chewed it into cud, and then I chewed the cud. Digesting, digesting. A very physical process. It all became part of my bones and my blood.

It also became my poetry and my prose. This was therapeutic for me, but problematic. I was using stories that were not my stories. They belonged to my clients. My clients had a right to confidentiality. I could not bite off bits of therapy, chew them into poems, pseudo-fiction, essays, and make my writing public. More and more I wanted to make this writing public. I felt forced toward fiction. I got part way there. What I found along the way were some things that seemed a bit like terrible archetypes to me, quintessential details, typical scenarios from the world of child abuse. I picked these up and held them in my hands. They would do. I did not need to tell the story of any particular client. Nor did I need to imagine totally original material. I could use the details that came repeatedly from client after client; or from my reading; or from my dreams. The essence of the early writing would be this: how such details changed and shaped themselves as they made their way through me onto the page—and how I placed myself in this new written world that came from what my clients showed to me. My sense of wonder, perhaps oddly, would inform the early poetry and prose.

Later, the writing would take a turn toward my own peculiarities, my limitations, my crankiness as a therapist and as a person. I wasn't always happy with my clients or myself. Difficult moments in the therapy relationship would appear in the poetry and in the prose. Again, I found what seemed almost archetypal and used it freely, creating details, shifting things to shape them differently.

So this collection takes the raw material of my life, particularly my life as a therapist, and transforms it. The "characters" here—both the clients and the therapist—are rooted in the real, but changed. The changes are sometimes strange, off-center. The whole that emerges is not meant to be an accurate reflection of reality. When you read this collection, you might get the impression that all of my clients were severely traumatized in the most dramatic ways, that every therapy hour was filled with tales of horror, that my clients were routinely turning into three-year-olds or seven-year-olds in the middle of a sentence. In fact, most of the time my work life was commonplace, satisfying, quite wonderful, and not at all overwhelming. Even a session with a client who had multiple personality disorder (now officially called dissociative identity disorder) would, on an ordinary day, look ordinary. We would be two adults sitting in a room having a conversation. We might be talking about how the client was going to handle a difficult relationship with a co-worker; or how she was going to motivate herself to exercise; or how she could manage her panic attacks more easily. When you read this collection of writings, you will have an altogether different impression. Trauma, until it is metabolized, distorts. This is true for the trauma survivor; it is also true for her therapist. With time, and a great deal of work, a new and more balanced perspective is found— by the client and by her therapist.

I could not write this collection now. I am not newly impassioned, radically challenged, or just plain scared in the way I was some years ago. As I write in the Epilogue, even the most terrible trauma, even the most dramatic aftereffects of trauma, have become "common" for me. I love the word "common." Since my early involvement in the Women's Liberation Movement, this word has been associated with a quote from Judy Grahn: "The common woman is as common as the best of bread / and will rise." I think of myself as having been mixed and kneaded and punched and heated over and over by years of trauma work. The horror that my clients endured no longer takes center stage for me. The switch from one personality to another no longer carries a special jolt of electricity. I work with more equanimity now, and the ordinary humanity of my clients is what amazes me.

That is today's truth. Tomorrow could surprise me.

Memory

In this collection of writings, you will find images of bizarre and gruesome forms of child abuse. You might wonder if such things really happen. You might wonder if I, as a therapist, give credence to the more extreme examples of what my clients tell me. There is no easy or simple answer to these questions.

Sometimes the images that emerge in trauma therapy have a brilliant, surreal quality and a radical lack of context. They emerge raw, without the shaping that comes from grounded thinking. Some of these images—presented as the client's memories—are obviously *not* accurate reflections of what I call, for lack of a better term, "objective reality." I have heard clients complain of body parts missing, of deafness, of blindness—clients who sat with me, clearly physically intact, able to hear or see just ten minutes before. We therapists have a vocabulary to help us handle such material. We can speak of psychosis, delusion, hysteria, fabrication, attention-getting behavior, introjection, incorporation, fragmentation, primary process thinking, symbolization, failure to symbolize, concrete thinking, traumatic thinking, programmed thinking, screen memory, dissociation, trance logic, and on and on. Or we can sit still and listen. Sometimes, later in the therapy, things change. The deafness becomes a child personality's need not to hear the unbearable; and, later, the whole person's need to deny the unacceptable. The missing body part becomes a threat of mutilation made in circumstances of terror; or an internalization of what the client witnessed when too young or too frightened to distinguish self from other; or a dream; or a way to say "I live in pieces."

Other information, equally surreal, equally bizarre, might in the end seem to reflect objective reality. If a relatively coherent story has been put together, if no alternative interpretation seems more convincing, and if the client becomes more able to cope with her life, that is usually good enough for her and certainly good enough for me. I don't know how to sort the "real" from the "unreal" with any finality, unless corroborating evidence is found. Human beings are capable of surreal, bizarre, sadistic, gruesome cruelties. We know this. I know this now more surely than I knew it before my clients began to teach me.

In the mid-eighties, when the first of these collected writings came into being, we trauma therapists did not speak much about the nature of memory. In recent years, it sometimes seems we speak of nothing else. We have been forced to move beyond an early simplicity expressed in the slogan "Believe the client."

That simple stance of believing the client was corrective. Before the trauma movement of the 1980's, psychotherapists were strongly influenced by the later work of Sigmund Freud with its tendency to interpret all childhood traumatic material out of existence. For the late Freud, all was fantasy. In reaction, for those of us who believed in the reality of child abuse, almost all was fact.

Time passed. We listened more carefully, and longer, to our clients. We honored our own desire to do work that was as careful and thoughtful as we could make it. We were pushed by abuse-denying forces, such as the False Memory Syndrome Foundation, toward greater clarity. We had time to think. The result, now, is a more complex view of abuse histories. Trauma memories, many of us have come to believe, are as likely to be inaccurate as other memories. And as likely to be accurate.

I myself cannot recreate the last week of my own life reliably. Additions, exaggerations, deletions, minimalizations, and distortions will creep in, no matter how hard I try to "tell the truth." On the other hand, when I speak of the events of the past week, I expect my listener to accept the basics. If I say I went to San Francisco last week, then I did go to San Francisco last week. If I say I had cheesecake for dessert last Wednesday, it is likely I had cheesecake, but it is also likely that the day I ate the cheesecake was Tuesday. If it becomes important to determine whether it was Wednesday or Tuesday, I will gather as much context as I can around that cheesecake, and try to set it in time more clearly. I might or might not be accurate in my conclusion. My mundane memory is both reliable and unreliable. Traumatic memory now seems much the same to me.

So, do I believe these gruesome stories of child abuse? Here is my answer today: I do not consider it my job to determine whether the story reflects objective reality. I wasn't there, after all; and I am a therapist, not an investigator. On the other hand, I generally accept the basics. However, I do not get attached to any element of the story. I know the details might change and story will probably evolve. For the purposes of therapy, what is important is the meaning of the story to the client; what is important is the use the client makes of the story in her life in the present, how it helps her and how it hurts her. For large parts of the typical trauma therapy, the details of abuse are not even referred to. What we talk about is how the client's life is going: can she do the things she wants to do? has she developed patterns of behavior that hinder her? how can she think or feel or act differently so that her life works better? Garden variety therapy is the norm, but you wouldn't know that from this collection of writings. This collection, as I said, sprouted from a very particular soil.

Writer's Note

A significant portion of the writing that follows portrays women working as clients in therapy. These are literary creations and none is intended to represent any actual person. Trauma histories and reactions to these histories are also fictionalized—but are meant to convey something of the essence of what one therapist has heard in the course of her work with many survivors of childhood abuse.

Prologue

Autumn

It is autumn, glint-edged and intricate,
and I am home again. This year the change
begins as outline: bright red, bold
orange on the farthest branches.
A bulk of green stays on from summer, strong
and central, clean. However odd and striking,
the colors side by side are simply there.
Nothing pale or weakened, nothing tentative.
No irony, no paradox, no riddle to be solved.

All living is transition, form to form.
We suffer or create our metamorphoses.
We hate or love or are ambivalent.
We fail in many seasons; not always.
This year in autumn I am home and happy.

This year I have remembered old abstractions—
goodness, truth, beauty; and
my current favorite, the will to live.
I take them back, but alchemized,
solidified, and rounded by the roll of years.
I hold them as a child holds stones for luck
against a world not safe. They comfort me.

1

Poetry: introductions

Unfinished

I was a child contained and careful,
cautiously enshelled. But I believed
my world was roomy. For did not Truth
stand large with classic lines against one wall?
And was not Love just soft enough for sitting
near the window as I read? What could be
more spacious than the ancient house of Faith?
Containment not yet named remained invisible.

I grew up and, growing, cracked the shell
I had not known was there. All form fell from me.
I traded Truth for existential risk, stood on bare air.
I breathed excitement for my breakfast every day.
I was thin and sure and freer than before.
I did not notice how abstraction
had replaced abstraction in my life,
how all was white on white,
how some connection still to some reality
had simply not been made.

Nor did I notice this:
that evil never thins to absolute abstraction.
Even weakened it is substantive, embodied.
Even ghostly it is cold and can be touched.
More to the point, it could touch me.

As If It Were a Dream

i.

Grandpa had flowers, I remember now.
He let me pinch the snapdragons, gently.
They opened, they closed,
they were yellow, they were white.
I had no garden of my own.
I dug in somewhere, though; labored, loved;
found clean sharp tools; grew things.
The things I grew were sentences perhaps.
Or did I cultivate a self in fact
and was I after all unique as well as Catholic?
Tentative: now there's a word.
Tenacious is another.
I held on to Truth for quite some time.
I see it now—triangular, translucent.
No color there, I note. An aspect lacking.

Meanwhile there was the question of evil.
I confess I was suspicious.
Could evil be the matrix of every deepest color?
I thought it could.
And if it was, how things turned inside out!

I looked around for evil.
I poked in dusty corners of the attic.
I searched the cellar not quite honestly.
I was ambivalent. I let years pass.

I know now evil is a messy thing,
and utterly specific. It has its colors, yes,
as limited as voices are when they can only scream
or whisper, ineffective, in the wind.

ii.

The story could be told
as if it were contained,
as if it were a dream.
It could begin like this—

One night in solid middle age
agnostic and plain as pea soup
I was ushered into a white room,
instructed to sit on a straight-backed chair;
instructed to watch and to listen.

Hairy fingers entered infant openings.
Young bodies were kept cold and shaking.
Laughter rattled, echoing like tin
against clean white walls.
Here was the smear and the feel
of various viscous materials.
Blood, semen, feces. Vomit—
Rot, and the smell of that.
I could breathe if I so chose.
I was free to consider colors.
I was advised against staying too long.

I left but I went back;
those cold young bodies had amazing eyes.

This is a dream;
I can tell it this way.

I got off the chair
and I sat on the floor
and I watched and I listened
and time passed.
I was alone with the children and their eyes—
kaleidoscopic shows of terror,
pale blue absences,

pearl-green moments of hope,
depth and flatness, heat and cold—
inside those eyes the pieces of the splintered souls
would come and go.
I saw colors then I had not seen before.

Here is the odd part.
I sat on the floor with the leavings of evil
and I stayed clean.

One night recently I had a real dream.
The stuff of my brain got sucked backwards.
Perhaps there was a tornado pulling at my skull.
I remember the dark green air,
Winona, Minnesota,
my sometime childhood summers.
The family trooped to the cellar,
stayed in the southwest corner,
waited for the radio to say the danger had passed.
In the dream the danger did not pass.
My brains under pressure were buckling.
Terror grew in the thick green mass.
Each action I attempted was fragile.
I watched myself slip on the surface of my shiny mind
and fall.

But in the make-believe dream,
remember,
I stayed clean.

To Follow

To follow with shorted breath
the impulse—
having felt separate threads wind to rope,
to pull myself hand over hand
across the chasm,
dizzy and exhilarated,
knowing the rope's thickness but not
how it is anchored.

As If

As if language were the hook that caught the fish,
dangled it out over water,
the blue air behind,
some breeze,
a modest rising sun,
and no onlookers;

just so,
sure of the deadly, useful core the task contains,
she casts a line to catch the thing
and waits.

The Notebook

She dropped it on my
ink-stained,
refinished,
little
captain's desk.
(The top lifts up like
gradeschool memories.
Bookshelves are built in.)

It was a well-used spiral notebook,
its cover red and creased,
its full pages fat.
"Read the last bit," she said.
"I didn't write that."

I bent and read the notebook's long last paragraph.
A saucy, taunting (furious) second self
rumbled loud against the flattened page,
language pumping up like women at the Y
sweating on their backs and building muscles.

The full moon kept me company all night.

Morning brought me coffee, hot and dark.
Until then I had only known the single self.
I pondered cups lined up along my open kitchen shelf.
Cups can contain, have brims.

Dark clouds in the distance
I noted as I drove to work.

9

Two

Against a great canvas   that tough cloth
she lays with a flat knife   lapis lazuli
hard ground for blue, precise.
Sharp sorrow here, darkness disguised.
Self-making from stone dust
with cold daybright water.

I have seen this woman strut and glitter,
blazon forth. She shines and she can shatter.
I am private, practical, stubborn as rope.
I hold what I intend to hold.

She has fibers, too; hers have been tested—
stretched and pressed as mine have not.
And she survives: a brightly-colored being
who casts a sharp, dark shade.

I have my colors, drawn from
sources less severe.
I am absorbing every hour faithfully
a hue, a tone. I work at it.
Some minutes of some days
the whole damned
spectrum seems to fit
inside my soul.
Those days I carry colors
like liquid in a bowl.

I think she cannot comprehend
a thing so whole
as my unbroken bowl.
Nor can I know the wilder colors
out beyond the spectrum—

all the edges of the pieces
of such a soul as hers.

We meet by miracle, I am aware.
So far we make a decent working pair.

Katherine

i.

All up and down the street they wanted sex.
Young Katherine wanted love, took sex instead
and sewed it secret places
in the garments of her grade school wardrobe.
The year was 'fifty-nine,
the place, the USA,
but she was a wartime child,
her pockets filled with contraband.
She had their names and whether they wore underwear;
they had imaginings of manhood
and Katherine's guilt to hide their own.
They were too many males, too similar.
They took too much.
They cut the pieces of her girlhood far too small.

Then came Blaine, unlike the others.
He wore a golden look and shook
the center of her early teenage soul.
He held her whole for a while.
In the lined palms of his large hands
she curled up, special as a rescued bird.
The love made up for the sex almost.

Blaine had a father grown old and dry.
The father died as fathers will.
Blaine shined his shoes and wore a tie
and drove all night to the funeral.

He came back seeking Katherine
and found her.
Into the young vagina
he gently wedged a stick
and told her with a whisper,

kissing her,
the stick was dynamite.

He held a match in his hand.

He / held her mind / in his hand.

For a mind held as hers is held
nothing intervenes between
idea and reality.
Threatened, the event occurred.
Her girl core forever torn,
her mind eternally explodes.

Also, her mind did not explode.
Here, as everywhere for Katherine,
reality was varied, split, elusive, and complex.
She multiplied her mind that day times three,
needing the numbers,
needing places to be free
of fondness for beloved Blaine.

The brain remained,
material for mad potters of the alleyway,
friends of Mama.
Now Katherine's mind was held
in the hands of seven males.
These new men had drugs
and muscles
and a circle to provide.
Inside the circle was a place to hide.
Some days they only drank and joked
about her tender pubic hair.
She was their queen, they said,
mighty pretty, mighty fair.
She blushed, pubescent and confused.

Some days they were ambitious,

got out ropes and whips.
She was the center of the holy ritual.
She would be tested by the holy act of rape.
Her body would be bruised
and her mind would be shaped
by the hands of the seven,
friends of Mama.

The clay they played with—
Katherine—
seemed malleable enough.
They twisted, pulled, and knotted up her brain
until the perfect form of pain
was stunningly achieved.
Inside they left long twisted trails of vacancy,
like corridors for crawling through.
So Katherine crawled along distorted corridors
inside her lonely mind
and begged for pieces of reality to eat.
Her take each day was sparse, a crumb or two.

She thinned,
she paled,
she bent.
she never grinned.
Like this, she could not qualify for queen.
They told her she was damned,
but could be saved by them
and punishment.

Just once she tried to tell.
Her mother looked confused and sipped her gin,
then spoke of how it's nice to have a lot of men.
Young Katherine multiplied herself again.
She didn't feel right, being bent and thin.

The several selves acquired names and clear-cut tasks.
A life like Katherine's needed managing.

Kate kept track of daily obligations.
Rina handled sex. Trina took the pain.
Thor was large and silent. He held the sacred rage.
Sister played by flashlight in a pocket of the mind.
Angel was the spirit, never broken.

Katie was the youngest child;
her eyes were always open.

ii.

The therapy demands a certain skill.
Some days we work like welders, sparks flying.
We use large gloves and headgear,
we hold our torches steady.
We respect the spurt of fire,
the danger to both of us,
and the necessity.

Some fires cannot be controlled by skill.
Think of a forest, the rage of red
heat sweeping through, the terror.
Afterward, black charring. Later, though,
improbable green shoots: Katherine's; mine.

I am embarrassed to speak as plainly as I must.
This is my own fire, caught from hers.
A green surprise of passion,
supple, young and holy,
old and wild and strong.

Strange colors, these.
Such a scarlet violence.
Such a tender verdancy.
The clash of hue and tone unsettles me.
Is this a nightmare or a dream (and whose)?

Have we the mix of things to make a vision here?
This would be strictly Old Testament,
stern and thorough,
all magic shrouded darkly
or in light too bright to bear:
divinity not yet made human.

It is written:
God came once in a burning bush.
A sacred conflagration
and a full, green foliage
can coexist.
The bush was burning
but not burned.

Poetry: reversals

Once Upon a Time Can Be Reversed

i.

I've heard of worlds turned inside out,
the seams exposed, the underside
of knots and loose ends hanging;
in such a world the patterns are all coded,
clear to those who know the craft,
to outsiders obscure.

In such a world lives Cora's grandmother.
Let's picture her:
the rocking chair and white, white hair,
the fireplace, the shawl of lace,
the knitting with a many-colored skein.
We will not ask what memories remain
inside the brain that watches rain
fall gently on the window pane;
we will not ask but we will know
the things the knitting will not show
because the patterns are reversed
in every detail
as rehearsed
long years ago
and in another place.
Each color has a counterpart, concealed.

Each stitch hides messages that cannot be revealed.
This woman rocks to rhythms she can't hear,
has visions she can't bear,
and whispers in her sleep:

Beware!
Beware of everything you keep;
dig deep—
and far out in the field;
dig deep—
and day will never yield
what you have buried in the dark.

My little pretty, hark!
Sweet little pretty, hark!

ii.

Last year I collected formerly rejected old abstractions.
I have them in my pocket now
and would not give them up.
I like the solid feel of honesty and grace.
I like the texture of an antique courage all restored.
I like the firmness of some temporary separations:
will from impulse,
idea from emotion,
there from here and
then from burly now.
The clarity goes through me coolly
like fresh lemonade or
like a deep breath after apnea.
The sureness settles
like a long-forgotten blessing
dropped lightly as farewell
before I can object that I no longer have
the faith I had back then.
And so I pocket that slight blessing here with all the rest.

What harm?

But going into the sharp wind today,
my breath abruptly taken from me,
the need to lean far forward just to keep some balance
overcoming any drive toward dignity,
I had to laugh. If I now put my hand into that pocket
just to touch a bit of the surviving mind I kept there,
I'd make myself a thin and spinning object of the wind,
my elbow out,
my teacup shape
quite caught—
and fraught with such fragility
that I, as I myself,
would surely scarcely any longer be.
And being is the thing,
the inmost spring of the thing,
without which,
naught.

Yes!
Being is beneath the skirt of all the rest:
central, like sex;
dark
or shining;
private or promiscuous;
corporeal or rooted in the mind;
a viscous bit of sticking stuff
or quick or bright as instant liberation
which, like magic, can be holy or obscene.

O magic can be holy or obscene
and I have known a bit of both this year.

The large plain land of moderation
where I took root and grew for many years,
where grasses bend with God's great breath,
where sun is regular and easily remembered,

is a place without a need for either kind.
But I have been with those who live elsewhere.

iii.

I have been with those
who toss the fragments of the mind into the air
and tell the future by the bells all ringing there;
whose dreams become reality
with themes of circumstantiality
professionally played beyond the stage
of nightmares which, when prettied up for telling,
become visions for the audience, compelling
without smelling of the urine or the feces
or the sexual excretions
or the terror on the breath
or the bloody ritual death.

It is not politic
to stick the viewers to the quick,
to show them things unseen
without the sheen of wonder
and the stagy sound of thunder.

These are rules from stranger schools
than I had ever known;
but I was shown
how magic, all unwanted, can become
as daily as a loaf of bread;
how cuts upon the head will heal
from Cousin's thumb
making crosses upside-down;
how toys ten feet away will shake themselves alive
and walk to those
who watch their power playing games
against their better sense;
and how the sacred thread of sheer survival

binds the spirit to the fabric
which is backdrop to the being
of the one who sits with me,
who must be seen.
And that is magic too.

iv.

The children know the crematorium,
the hot red roar of it,
and how the bodies get thrown in.
The children know and they will never tell
about the sound, about the smell,
about the power and the spell
the grownups in a circle cast
in one unholy din
while weaving, weaving, weaving
kin to kin.

Three crosses—
and the children watch them burn.
A large knife—
and the point is dripping blood.
Three coffins—
and the bodies in them: small.

The facts are spinning red to black to white,
a run of blood in firelight
around the circle of the night
where evil laughs at any right
the children have to innocent delight.

Their hands have held the sacrificial knife,
their fingers stick with infant ritual blood,
their tears fall red against the rule of life,
their minds divide as young minds never should.

v.

Was there once upon a time a single mind
turning like a crystal in the light?
And did the hammer hit the crystal mind
with one or many blows before it split—
a facet flying at a white, blank, wall,
another landing on a bare wood floor,
a third embedded in a cushion's safe dark crease,
a fourth hurled out a window into night?

And others,
many others,
still in flight.

vi.

I dream my own brain in a box
with labels: Do Not Drop.
The thing is tough, but not uncrackable;
resistant,
there,
invisible,
and utterly substantial. And I
am microscopic. I can go into.
I can fly out of.

Awake, I would take kinesthetic hold,
get my hands around the thing and cup it,
catch its nature. This is a loving longing,
lonely. I would know my only mind.

I must because she can't, yet,
hers being split into many
(this is not a metaphor)
parceled by pain
(this is not a metaphor)

each mind wrapped in brown paper and twine
saved from years previous
(this is metaphor, but barely)
the paper wrinkled, creased, worn and
paradoxically, simultaneously
fresh, crisp as the day the thing needed packaging,
covering, hiding,
saving,
(o precious pain);
each piece of self, preserved, sweet, named, and secret
and none of this is
metaphor.

vii.

Knowledge is a thing with many faces,
one behind the other;
not like masks,
not separate like that.
There is more blend, more fuse,
more chance you lose
the things you think you know,
more getting caught in ones or twos
forgetting what the many faces show.
I mean that I had known before,
that hints and hunches
made me know with fragile certainty
and then erase the thing I surely knew
and then replace what got erased.
My mind became a mirror
of the holy or unholy war
in Cora.

I caught epiphanies
of revelation, interdiction,
interwoven fact and fiction,
all presented carefully

in doses of deliberate titration,
but whose reaction,
hers or mine,
was being tested for,
I could not tell.

Then finally I knew:
that she/that they/that all the singular plurality
contained within one flesh —
the many personalities,
the young, the old,
the crowded, hostile, brave and fearful,
strong and funny, thoughtful, cheerful personalities,
all warring, yet connected by the tissues of the past —
that they/that she
whose single body shakes with unremembered memories
in session after session of this agonizing work
was once a child controlled by those
who worship Satan;
was once a child,
her mind and body victimized
in ways as various as multi-faceted reflections
of the whole of human virtue, turned, reversed;
was once a child,
saw other children killed,
and may herself have killed;
was once a child
and sang the chant
and held the knife
and drank the blood
and ate the flesh of human infants
slain for sacrifice.

viii.

They wait inside the body,
each personality separate, alone.

24

Some sit, some lie curled and fetal;
some would run screaming; some would pace;
some would think; some would joke;
all are bound today:
ropes of hope
and memory.

A free flying out is wanted,
an agony of wishing,
twinned, turned inward.
Here is the multiple coupling of real and unreal,
an ancient impossible puzzle of shapes;
she must separate these, using no force,
remember herself.

Here mixes clear dark with clear light;
the two combine and hold,
black bird and gull under a white moon—
reflections, connections—
sweet silly song of the loon—
wave after wave after wave.
No muted color could survive this scene.

She would cut the artery
for the spurt of it, but doesn't.
Gently, precisely, she cuts into her
arms, legs, torso. Something comes out,
shows, is red: a delicate pattern of beading.
That's why they cut, these hurt ones;
even the slowest bleeding
shows.

ix.

I am the therapist.
My task is in the aftermath. I watch

while she who was broken in childhood
sorts through the pieces,
matches irregular edges,
finds the old picture,
attempts to resemble herself.

x.

It is important to say
just what it is
you are talking about
even if the meaning
slips a bit
after you say it.
I believe in telling relevant fact.
Something bright might emerge,
might stand, in the end.

Meanwhile, I have visions of mercury,
small balls of it rolling here, rolling there,
uncollectible; and blood
where broken glass
cut the skin.

xi.

Long ago thermometers were whole
and could be read by each two-tenths degree.
The swelling heat contained itself,
clean glass under the tongue,
someone's hand on someone's hot forehead.
No more.

This is a time of broken things.
All is spillage in a moist dark place.
Caution to those who travel here:

sharpness; rotting; caustic waste.
Terror to those who travel here:
rats, bats, spiders, snakes.

Cora has descended into hell.
In the third year will she rise
and roll the stone back home?
She is the child of darkness now
and cannot see and cannot come to comfort
on a soft blue couch.

I tell her Look around,
I tell her You are here
where teddy bears are sitting on the floor
and baby dolls and small green cars
and crayons and a safe, locked door.
But she is in another land
and she sees blood on her left hand.

Pressure cookers hold a deadly steam.
Hers held for many years,
the pressure many pounds.
Loving mothers tell their daughters:
hold the old steel cooker under cold and running water;
do not lift the lid
until the gauge reads Safe.
Cora has no gauge to say how many pounds,
when to let the steam,
what genies might get free,
how civilized, or not, they'll be.
So Cora's hot release is barely safe enough.
The steam like hissing sounds.

xii.

One cool day the mountains called to her.
She climbed up and stood and took the wind.

Inside, the child parts jumped and sang and grinned
for feeling good as children should
from time to time.

Whoosh! came the clean strong wind inside
and swept the floor and sent them
giggling, sprawling, whirling,
never minding just that once
that suddenly there was no place to hide.

Whoosh! came the clean strong wind inside
and mixed them all together in a happy blend,
arms and legs and memories,
heads and hearts and referees
and inside seemed so wide—
so wide—
that all the world's winds could abide
and Cora still contain the tide
come swelling up the mountainside
and in addition could decide to ride out all her time.
She would ride her whole damn time
whether reason, whether rhyme.

Before she left she cried.
For joy and tiredness she cried
and climbed back down the mountainside.

xiii.

Every being turns its inside out.
Every being tumbles upside-down.
Once upon a time can be rehearsed
and then for fun or
for salvation
once upon a time can be reversed.
Think of umbrellas.
Think of pockets.

Think of the grandmother rocking away
and Cora the grandchild
who sits on the floor
watching the soft blur of colors
all spun in the whirl of the top
she has just learned to use.

This is the daytime that follows the night.
This is the grandmother of the daylight.

This is the time of forgetting,
of pumping the top
to get it to spin and
loving the blur that it makes.

Now think of Cora years later
unlearning the blur.
Colors differentiate.
Here is red and red is blood, of course;
and red is blood through years of nights
until and finally this red will liberate itself
for apples and pimentos,
for red bikes and sunsets—
or suddenly appear as accent in a favorite work of art.

On good days she will see the world this way,
each thing itself. Not all days will be good
and many things she sees will hold old terrors
in their back pockets. She will not be surprised.
She has walked the streets
and knows about the range of pockets
and all they can contain.
She has walked the streets in icy wind
and sheer sunlight
and, lovingly, in rain.
In rain she carries all her pain
like packages inside her mind
but both her hands are free

and I can see her running, arms outstretched,
into the windy rain beside the sea.

O I can see her running, running, running
into the windy rain beside the sea.

Prose:
the therapist
at work; and after work

Hearts

Perhaps there really was a group of people devoted to terror, worshipping terror; a group now almost certainly dispersed to the outer edges of the universe, participants either dead or so totally changed as to be unrecognizable; a group to whom disguise was integral, and still is.

And perhaps the group did exactly this: cut open the chest of an adolescent girl (was she rebellious?) and directed a small child, also a girl, to hold in both her small child hands the heart, still beating, of the girl whose chest was cut open, the blood vessels intact, the blood pumping nicely, so that it was like holding a frightened bird, and it felt like a privilege.

And perhaps this small child, the privileged one, grew up and came to speak to me, whispering, for it was a secret. She would have the body of a grown woman by this time. She would be wearing Oshkosh overalls and a deep purple silk blouse with billowing long sleeves. She would be a big woman, muscled, with large rough hands; a worker. Also a painter, a sculptor, a psychic, and most of the time a lesbian. There would be room in the wardrobe for multiple expressions.

This grown woman blinks and rolls her eyes upward. She slides from the couch of my therapy office to the floor. She lands efficiently, crosslegged. She looks at me and asks, in a deep voice I know from sessions past—it belongs to a male protector, long won over, a gay male of the butch sort, who was threatening at first, but that was a long time ago—she/he asks *Are you ready? Are you sure?*

By this signal I know there is something to tell that is regarded as difficult.

The legs shift up. The knees are grabbed and held for life. The whole body seems to shrink, but it is only compression caused by fear. The head turns up and looks toward me, for I am still in my chair and she is still on the floor. The wink comes. Here is the seven-year-old, then. Been practicing that wink for three months and has it pretty much mastered. A pale grin. She likes me, but she is frightened of her task. She tells me about the held and beating heart. She tries to make sure I understand the wonder, how special it is to hold a heart; and how secret it is.

I am almost used to this sort of image. I can almost enter the world in which such things become an honor. As long as I give no thought at all to the girl whose chest is used for such an event, I can approximate equanimity.

And, of course, it is perhaps entirely imagination, this scene. After all, this same woman sometimes turns into a nine-year-old of undetermined sex whose tongue has been cut out. Since the woman speaks very well, and easily, before and after she becomes this nine-year-old, I conclude there is something other than my kind of reality at work. I have theories about this sort of thing, not all of which involve delusion, not all of which involve terror, not all of which involve abuse, but I do not worry about them while I listen on this day.

Listening is the task, so I keep listening. Now comes a new level of wonder. The eyes open wide and shine. The necessary history, the big secret, so dangerous to disclose, is out. Now comes the part of the job for which the seven-year-old personality of the forty-four year-old woman has unadulterated enthusiasm. She has figured it out, in consultation with her internal friends, other personalities. They have figured it all out. They know the solution to their Big Problem. They have remembered the heart once held in their child hands and now they know how to help their own hurting heart.

I cannot tell this today without using the plural. The woman's reality is plural and will not always be collapsed toward normalcy.

Their own hurting heart, then—the heart of the woman who is both multiplied and divided, who feels herself to be so many that she cannot on one day achieve a good count; this heart has gotten tired of agony and it wants to stop. But the seven-year-old and her internal companions, the ones in her little group, know that if the heart stops, they all die; and death has long been the enemy. So this young personality tells me the plan: they will cut their own chest open, take their own hurting heart in their own loving hands, and make it feel better. The blood vessels will remain attached. *It is very safe, Shirley, nobody dies. Don't worry.* She smiles. She is proud.

There is a lot of work to do before the end of the session. The need to heal the hurting heart is real, and requires acknowledgment. Next, safety must be attended to. A coterie of older personalities agrees to be responsible: if there is one tiny movement toward the chest with a sharp object they will take over; they will go to the hospital if necessary. I trust the plan. We have made other plans for safety in the past and safety has been maintained.

Whatever else we do before we say good-bye this day evaporates for me. Do we work to make the trauma story bearable? Now how would we do that, exactly? Do we work toward less alarming methods for healing hurting hearts? If we do, they can't compete with what the seven-year-old self proposed. In the end we do what we always do: we make an appointment for the next week.

Sessions similar to this have actually happened in my practice as a psychotherapist. A session such as this could have happened. And if it did, in the middle of the night, unable to sleep, I might have written a letter to a friend—call her Annie. I would tell her about my day, about the session with the woman in the Oshkosh overalls and the purple silk blouse, and then I would go on—

Annie, this damned heart image gets to me.

I have lots of days when I am nicely grounded, able to think and feel and respond like a whole person, well-trained, professional and human at the same time. I also have days when extreme horror seems somehow absorbable. This is perhaps weird, but necessary if the work is to go on. The flip side of that absorbability (is there such a word?) shows up when I can't get it at all—when what is being told to me just sits meaningless in my mind; or on my mind. Water beading on a waxed car.

Once in a while, like now, I turn suddenly unprotected. Can't simply listen; can't absorb; can't shed. No Turtle Wax. Just raw exposure.

So what got to me? I think my client found a way to meld the various aspects of her reality to each other. Some separation slipped away. She got fusion, as in nuclear physics. The impulse to do serious harm to herself just melted into the impulse to love and heal her own heart and an explosion occurred in <u>my</u> psyche—as if this woman found an archetypal way to speak of the confusion of self-harm and self-healing that I observe day after day in so many survivors of intense abuse; observe and handle. But I can't handle this; at least not with any skill.

I can still see these little hands holding this little heart—

I can imagine the gentle way she holds and comforts her own hurting heart—

Maybe it was simple kindness that got to me.

34

As I write, I realize there is nothing for me to do with this except what I am doing. I now have this thing to hold. I can write to you about it, but the image will not go away and I am not even sure that I want it to. I think I need to hold it and turn it slowly in my own hands as if it were a sort of sculpture—see the love and the danger and the confusion; see the possibly historical roots of that cut-open chest; and feel the contours of the client's need to imagine that the path of self-harm is the way to healing. I just want to hold it all—as one moment of one woman's complex reality.

Thank you for listening, Annie. Write when you can.

By the way, when I asked this woman, many months ago, for permission to write to you, she looked at me sideways: "That lady a person of wisdom?" I said "Yes." She said "OK, write to her a lot."

Love—

P. S. Well, there was more to do. A long, deep cry. Then I started to think. What strange mental territories we enter. What would it take to get to a heart? You would have to contend with the rib cage. I think I read somewhere how much strength it takes to hold ribs apart, how protected real hearts are.

P. P. S. Remember those Holy Cards we got in grade school when the nuns were pleased with us? Remember the ones with pictures of the Sacred Heart, the saccharine Jesus, his chest opened to expose a thorn-surrounded bleeding heart? No wonder I can do this work with equanimity, most of the time—I was desensitized in the first grade.

Also, no wonder I slip off my patch of ground once in a while and find myself in the void; and hope it's fertile. Somewhere near here, ungraspable, there must be meaning. I think of Wallace Stevens and his evanescent phrase, "blown sheen." My own heart pumps madly with gratitude. Is that too corny? Maybe. It's also too true.

35

Prose:
in which the therapist
imagines the mind of the client

The Voices of Lena

The character:

> *Lena: survivor of ritualized, sadistic childhood abuse; has multiple personality disorder (also called dissociative identity disorder)*

The personalities of Lena:

> *The Organizer: adult part of self whose task it is to keep the system of personalities working as smoothly as possible*
>
> *Leon: personality who acts as the power behind the scene; age unclear*
>
> *Magdalena: part of self who deals with the outside world most of the time; adult*

Maggie: adolescent part who suffers flashbacks to childhood abuse

Delly: latency age personality who is bulimic

Leonard: part of self who holds the worst traumatic memories; age unclear

Punch: young child personality

Babies: infant personalities

The Organizer

It was the whirl before again. Back in again. Pieces of each other mixing. The all color too brightness attacking.

Something is wrong. Getting up crooked. Something is wrong. All falling threatens.

Cracks everywhere.

Damn.

How is Magdalena managing this thing now? How is Maggie?

Try the old tack. Think theory. Structure. Grammar. Subject, object. No. Subject, verb, object. One thing after the other. Get your footing. Undeclared subject. Declare it. You get your footing. Yes. This is helping.

Next step: how is this helping? Please tell me. Undeclared you. Invisible you. Whoever you are, please you tell me.

Tell me what?

The lapses are coming faster. I have forgotten what I want you to tell me. And I see that you have become the indirect object. I am uncertain of just what.

Get your grounding. Work the grammar. Transform that adjective into a noun. Uncertain becomes uncertainty. Hmmm. Unfortunate choice. Makes not a thing but a chasm.

Well then give it a try. Attempt the leap. Over the chasm of uncertainty.

Or, what the hell, just fall in. Land in the chasm. Here we are. Located. Whoopee.

Observe here the territory of the radical uncertainty of. What? Of who is me. No. Is I. The radical uncertainty of who this particular I happens to be. Great, a complex possible subject. How about a verb? The radical uncertainty etc. rather frightens me. No. Frightens us. For we are plural here.

OK. Now try for something simpler. And more honest.

Here we are whirling and terrified again. Can't separate out. Like a washing machine, swishswish. Are we getting the dirt out? Too sudsy to tell.

Clever. But be more honest.

Too terrified to tell. Too terrified to tell this to anyone. Too terrified to understand what is happening. Understand. Stand under. Can't stand under, whole thing might drop on you. What whole thing? The undeclared whole thing. Can't stand, period. All the words are falling down falling down falling down. My fair lady. All mixed together and alone. Try hard with words. Words not working too much pain must not scream out loud remember this rule no screams allowed.

God I love my reality. We'd better have a meeting soon. If possible.

The Meeting

—She's asleep.
—Which one?
—Magdalena.
—Maggie.
—Both?
—Yes.
—Good. What the hell is going on lately?

—We don't know.

—Leon's not happy with the situation. Somebody must know something.

—It's the walls.

—Broken walls.

—Punch is walking around, trying to see out.

—I am *not*.

—She's everywhere except her room. Crouching. Jumping.

—Who's supposed to watch her?

—Watch who?

—Punch, you idiot.

—No one ever had to watch her before.

—I don't try to be all over the place. I don't want to. It's scary.

—Where is the scattering coming from? Come on, this is serious.

—It's that new job.

—Too many books.

—Words crowding the air.

—Hard to breathe.

—The library was supposed to be a good, safe job. Quiet. Magdalena could be around books all day, but not reading. Keep the stimulation down. That was the plan.

—Maggie's reading. And Magdalena can't breathe.

—Maggie's supposed to be able to read.

—She's reading bad stuff again.

—Jesus H.

—Throwing up all the time.

—Delly involved in that?

—I ain't!

—What exactly is Maggie reading?

—You don't want to know.

—I know!

—Shut up, Punch.

—I do. Black cover. Scary picture. Red. Knife.

—Leon must have picked it himself. Damn. When will he learn? He can't have that crap and have order, too.

—Maggie's scaring herself to death. Maggie's scaring *me* to death. But I ain't throwing up. Honest.

—Anybody noticed anything? Anybody from the outside?

—We don't think so.

—You know what this means.

—Maggie will cut herself up some. So what?

—More than that. Magdalena will take us to therapy again.

—Goddamn.

—We'll have to reinforce the walls.

—Dark again?

—I'm afraid so. And more screaming inside.

—I don't think Maggie can take that again.

—Have to.

—And the damn babies will cry day and night.

—Yes. Unfortunate.

—Too scary too scary too scary too—

—Shut up, Punch.

—You shut up.

—Come on, people. You know the routine. It's the walls or the hospital.

—Great choice.

—Tooscarytooscary—

—Get her out of here!

—What about names?

—Lena for therapy. Nothing but Lena. What's your name, Delly?

—My name is Lena.

—Good girl. Go tell Punch. Make sure she understands. All right, people, let's get to work. Not a chink in the wall when we're finished. No daylight. No exceptions.

Magdalena

Reason has been my rock; logic my preferred mode. This has appeared to be the prudent course, given certain

41

peculiarities in my experience. I am aware everyone does not live this way, so bound to the exigencies of the rational. To be honest, I wonder about my own capacity to continue to hold the course. Former certainties have begun to wobble, turn, whirl and blur: who I am, how I am, what I am, whether I am—these are things I no longer grasp. I hear the drama in such talk and dislike it. However a bit of the dramatic seems suddenly appropriate.

A small example might clarify things. Lately, the very act of walking from room to room has become an experiment. The data provided for this experiment are disturbingly unstable. This morning I wanted to go from the stacks to the reference room. I could not judge the level of the bare hardwood floor in the reference room as I approached. Its surface appeared unaccountably elevated. I retained some cognitive ability (a blessing, and not always the case) and recalled that I have a bit of experience with these tricks of perception. I chanced it and did not bend my knee or raise my foot to meet the shiny floor. I put my foot down bravely and, hallelujah, crossed the threshold without stumbling.

It has not always been this difficult to negotiate the physical world. I am a runner, a good one. I know the runner's high and can turn myself into the wind, rushing over surfaces of grass, gravel, tar, and asphalt, my feet holding and yielding in just the right places, adapting to each irregularity. Like a sensitive lover, perhaps; I have read about such things.

You will understand that these recent difficulties pose a challenge. I have begun, and this is not the first time, to question my sanity. I have taken appropriate steps and hired a therapist. She suggests there could be a link between my perceptual difficulties and the characters I see and hear in my rather too elaborate inner world. Her idea makes some sense, but only if I give credence to the characters—even to the point of allowing that they might have independent volition and some capacities of their own. Not a pleasant possibility.

I have asked myself: what if the therapist were right? If that short kid I see so often lately were looking through my eyes, trying to usurp my territory, influencing my perception, the floor would be—what? closer? more distant? I can work it both ways. As is usual. This despite my preference for the single level, the linear, the (currently receding, much longed for) logical, reasonable, rational.

This therapist says we might be approaching a diagnosis. It would be logical, reasonable, and rational to want to hear what she has to say.

Maggie

The flashes come: blood and pain, darkness and fire, nightmare demons, the white-walled room. A particle of a second per flash. A particle of self roused up, highlighted, lost. That's when it's easy, one piece at a time. Lately they often come crashing together. Light up the sky. Fourth of July. Free-eedom, free-dum, free-*dumb*.

The therapist says holding my breath and closing my eyes and clenching all muscles won't do. Always has, I say. Not if you want change, she says. Who wants change, say I. That part is bravado. And isn't.

We debate the issue inside, privately. What does *she* know? On the other hand, what *does* she know? Stalemate.

Take one deliberate breath, Lena, she suggests. Just one.

Ah, yes. Risk annihilation. Worse: risk hope. Worse yet: know that both will occur in a cosmic simultaneity. Tell yourself the anticipated bifurcated fate is preferable to the status quo. Use big words. And don't tell the bitch your name is Maggie.

One deep breath.

Deep is it, now? I am to admit into this situation a stream of air despite the near certainty that such a stream will be outrageously swollen, in full flood, all footing lost, nothing to grab. Right.

Right, says some smartass inside. Come on, people, let's just do the deed.

I'm trying. I actually am. I remind myself: to see, to know, to claim. It's like a mantra. Mantras are for calming, that's what they say. To See. To Know. To Claim.

One breath, the therapist prompts.

On purpose?

One breath, Lena.

Right out in the open?

One breath.

If you say so, Lady.

Delly

Leonard won't talk to that therapist lady. Won't dane, he says. Oh. Deign. Leonard don't have to. He's mostly in a separate place. We don't know him much. Except, when he comes we get squashed against the walls. He takes up all the room. He's got horns and green gunk on him. Once he came out all the way in the quiet room in the hospital. He bashed his head on the padded wall over and over and over and over. He never got the headache but we sure did. He hates it when we talk about him but we ain't scared about that no more. Here's a big secret about Leonard. He reads fat books. He takes the flashlight at night under the covers just like us but the words in his books are bigger and the sentences don't make a story. We would get tired just holding his books. Here's another secret. Leonard wears glasses. Nobody is supposed to know that one.

Leonard has things locked up inside him in a steel room with a big padlock, a major padlock like no one could ever get open even with a laser like on Star Trek. Leonard loves Star Trek. Once I found some writing Leonard wrote about the stuff in that room. It would make the world end if that stuff ever got out. Leonard won't let it out, though. One thing you can count on Leonard for, he won't spill the beans.

44

Punch

That lady pretends she can't see what goes on inside but I know she's lying. She says all she can see is the shell-body sitting on the floor with the teddy bears. She says she don't know until we tell. She says even if we tell she can't see inside. I don't believe she's that dumb. I'm just a kid and I can see lots of it. Even if she's blind she can feel the fire and hear the chanting. She's not blind. She sees other stuff like people being afraid even if they hide it good. She says there's a rule here about not hurting anybody and not killing anybody. We know better than to believe big people. Sometime we're gonna have to tell, though. We can feel it. We're just gonna have to tell. Even if we get all cut up for doing it.

Punch (later)

We told about the big knife and the special cup of blood. She didn't kill us. She said it was OK. We want to believe her. The big ones are saying we'll be sorry. She didn't laugh at us. She didn't whip us for lying. The big ones say the punishment will come later. They are stomping all around. They think maybe they better cut us up before somebody else does. They watched while we told. They waited in the shadow part by the wall and they let us tell. We never thought they would. The lady said it was OK. She said it was OK.

Excerpts:
from the therapist's journal

Everything was in place even down to several layers beneath the surface and then: the gap, the spot where the boards rot, or were never laid, or were laid like a trick, unattached. You fall through if you go there...

Responsibility is a mystery.

When I work with someone with multiple personality disorder, I tell her she is responsible for all of her actions. This is a mystery. I tell her she is responsible and my telling her this is a useful thing. She objects at first that she is unaware of many of her actions, that they are performed by other personalities. I tell her I know this. I say that she is, nevertheless, as a whole person, responsible for all of her actions. I might say this many times and it is as if I am building a platform, laying a board, nailing it down, laying another, another, another. There is more and more for her to stand on. The platform is words and the content of the words is essentially mysterious to her and to me. Still, she stands on the platform.

Perhaps this is no stranger than standing on a material platform constructed of wood. We all know that wood is made of molecules which are composed of atoms which are mostly space and not substance at all; and we stand on the wood with confidence.

My own responsibility as a therapist is more mysterious to me than the responsibility of my client. I have a job which can on some days be described simply: I stay there in my office. I offer listening, thinking, feeling; once in a while a learned technique; a lot of keeping my mouth shut; a lot of not imposing my reality; a dose of sharing my reality; many mistakes. I stay there as honestly and completely as I can on any given day. That's about it.

However. Sometimes this issue of responsibility crashes through the terrible, simple work of being there. The intensely suicidal client might be the occasion. Or the client who seems to gain nothing from therapy week after week. I try to think about my responsibility. I go to workshops on the legal and ethical aspects of being a therapist. I contemplate life and death; violence; and loneliness.

I believe I am at my best when I grasp the root—the radical responsibility each of us has for herself. So I steady myself with the thought that I am responsible *to* my clients but not responsible *for* them, no matter what the lawyers say. But even as I am holding to these basics, a vapor rises around me. *You fall through if you go there.* I wonder if I am failing to give due respect to mutuality, to community, to the influence we can have on each other. I question the very purity of the simple thought that each of us is responsible for herself. I confront my deepest wish to be magical, a whiz of a healer. I do not reach conclusions. I go back to work. Some client that week makes some progress. I can continue, a bit of faith under my feet. On such airy stuff we all stand, I suppose.

****

The writing workshop. Someone asked me Do you mean real eating of real human flesh? I answered, Yes.

But I did not simply answer yes. I made—meaning I constructed, painfully—a face. That face: meant to be apologetic, ameliorating. My whole social self was suddenly caught, trapped, embarrassed; these things are not said. Not when you mean them; not when they are not fiction. You don't talk out loud about children being involved in rituals where they see satanic sacrifice and eat flesh peeled from freshly killed babies; not in ordinary social settings; not if you believe this might have been the experience of someone you know.

The words I had put on paper to bring to the workshop, the sentences carefully formed, silently read, had provided distance. Now, with a direct question seeking a direct answer, we passed into a different frame. I passed into a different frame. Everything was suddenly immediate, real. I was the carrier of bad news. Shame dripped inside my social suit, like sweat. It was as if I had washed proverbial dirty linen, hung it to dry in the front yard on the day a wedding reception was scheduled right across the road. And the stains had not come out: blood and semen. Who wants to see that on a wedding day, the rest of the female world in white gowns and pink, innocent?

And imagine: if it had been my own experience...

* * * * * * *

My American Heritage Dictionary tells me that "memory" is from *smer:*
- •to remember sorrowfully (Germanic)
- •to mourn (Old English)
- •*Mimir:* a giant who guards the well of wisdom (Old Norse)
- •*memor:* mindful.

* * * * * * *

I am awake after bad dreams. I ponder the problem of intimacy with the abuser; the necessity of intimacy with the abuser. Victim and abuser share their most intense and secret times. Intense experience binds. Binds what to what?

49

I have inherited the dream of the child molested by her mother. The child is bound in a sheaf, her center constricted, her breathing impossible; one stick among many. Held this close she will never be seen. But they share a secret. Once at dinner, aged six, she dared to stare her mother down. Who saw whom? Was the father there?

I review my day. A woman shifts personalities as we are working in therapy. Now she is named for an Egyptian goddess. She is three years old, sweet and calm. She whispers, "I'm good. I eat everything." I wonder, trying to piece things together: *like Mama says?* Oh, the temptation to make a whole story. Fragments frustrate. Fragments are what we get.

She was a child and I was a child and we were both given flesh as a sacrament. Mine was sanitized, unleavened, given in daylight; and they said it was God. No one pretended for her that it was God. Her sacrament happened at cold night; was still bloody.

In my own night I ignore the echo of her words (*eat everything......everything......everything......*). I think general thoughts; about sacrifice, for example. The idea of sacrifice, holy or unholy, is not now in vogue. The idea of sacrifice is so universal, however, that it cannot be ignored. It is irrational and it comes from somewhere; fills some need. I was raised Catholic with Christ hung by nails and bloody before my eyes every morning at Mass, but I do not understand. My mind is five years old. How can horror make God happy? I can't get beyond this. Nighttime thinking has its limits.

****

Something transcendental keeps knocking at the edges of my life. It started—at least as poetry it started— outside: winter, Hide and Seek, cold, dark, the other kids running and screaming and I on my back in the hard-packed snow, staring at stars and making up a poem that I later wrote down. Seven years old. And that feeling:

vastness. The cold was important and how I could lie in it and not get chilled but be, rather, braced. This was in the city: Minneapolis, Minnesota. Concrete all around. It didn't matter—the wonder was above; and it must have been a moonless night.

And it comes now, this same feeling, in the very work of being a therapist, my daily bread, hour after hour sitting with one and then another and another person who reveals most often in the smallest doses but sometimes in an almost blinding burst: her pain—some thing which, exposed and awful (in the many meanings of that word, banal and sublime), seems to make room for a further depth of being; a settling or a tender emergence or, more rarely, a triumphant shout of being; a moment that seems holy if anything is holy; a sacred validation, an I Am.

Which is not just hers, which does not belong simply though it does belong primarily to the client. Which is shared. Witnessed. Held by both of us. That is the privilege.

And the many hours when the pain is present primarily in how the person will not, cannot, approach or even give a nod to it; the times of self-protection when all is covered over; the many trudging steps along the way, hot and crabby, when she—but I am tempted to follow, I do follow at times—becomes sure that there is no point: these are all part of it; perhaps the essence of it. I sit in myself and she in herself; connection forbidden. The temptation to be bored. The boredom overwhelming both of us on the worst days. And keeping going, coming back. Again. Again. And all of this essential. Like the long hike; the long poem; a whole life.

Like wiring the house that first winter when Ginny and I had only one small stove and no insulation; each bend of the wire being a challenge and my hands cold and slow and needing to be more exact than seemed possible and the long, long struggle, so many circuits, so many mistakes, the snap of the wire in the cold, its refusal to yield to the shape I needed from it and I never thought we

51

could do it, just the two of us with no experience and a book, paperback, costing less than ten dollars. And we kept on and here I am, computer running off that struggle. It's like that, too. Where is the transcendent in that? In this mood, this morning, I am inclined to reply: everywhere.

****

Working with multiple personality disorder gives— after the first years when all is focused on survival (mine, not the client's; hers too but right here I mean my own survival, my own ability to go on, to do something with what is given to me, hold it, put it down, not walk away from it, stay there at least in the vicinity and not be crushed out by the enormity; a process parallel to the client's)—ways to experience self and life, selflife, that are new or perhaps newly rediscovered having been (the parallel continues) covered over.

So that I imagine, finally, in the beginning of the seventh year of this work, my own separate selves—shyly but with anticipation of delight—coming out, young and eager and cautious, the scene is a rainy one, dark thick rain, and they have been thoroughly huddled under an umbrella, a black umbrella held by a well-meaning adult, no gender; and they come out not crawling, not on hands and knees, but also not standing up: hunched and moving; tentative with bent knees, bent necks, a bit stiff but it is clear that movement will help; they will stand up, look up, get wet in their new faces. All right. Let them.

Poetry:
of owls, mosquitoes,
dragons, and other things

Wisdom Symbols

Extract the well. Just pull it out of that old poem which
told too much anyway. Put an owl on the left side of the
stone rim. Reduce the element of bad ritual. Keep one
favorite line. Drop it slowly down—
They never knew how far the water was.

                    Here's what I'm really afraid of:
that owl might fly. Think of the wings, how you'd run.
He's a bird of prey, this symbol of wisdom,
Athena's bird, the motherless goddess
who by the way also lacked
a childhood.

              (The well smelled wet and stony, dark.
                   The well still smells. The well
                       and all wet places smell.)

Because you cannot give it up:
She never knew how far the water was.
She never knew.

Mosquito

Giles questions me: Where is the evil in
you? This writing paints you lily-white.
Where is the anger, at least? Are you
always the therapist, Shirley?

Zarod cautions me: Giles is right. All
binary pairs deconstruct. You won't get by
with innocence. Nor do you mean to.

i.

One little mosquito,
skittery and slim,
needs a drink of blood from me.
I shan't be bit by him.

Truth is, I don't mind
swatting his behind.

Which is all it takes, of course.

One bare hand,
quick and lightly tanned,
descends.

(Contact.)

(Smush.)

(Hooray.)

I can barely feel the corpse
I brush away.

ii.

I have been questioned:
your own persona here
is quite peculiarly pure,
they say to the therapist I am.

And oh they are right.
I am caught in my sweetness.
They are right, they are right.
I am caught in my sweetness.
I am caught in my sweetness, what a jam.

iii.

One way out is through the triangle.
Here is how I see it:
I take one point, second base let's say.
First base is the victim
and third is victimizer.
See? I'm equidistant. And nobody is home.

iv.

I can imagine being the perpetrator of horror
as easily as I can imagine being the recipient.
I kill little life forms almost daily through the summer
but that is not the point.

v.

(Killing me softly)—
I try for a trick of compassion—
a somewhat tanned
gigantic hand

descends.
(It can't feel the shape of my corpse as it brushes me off
but that is not the point. I can't feel *it* either.)

vi.

I don't get angry.
Do you hear me?
I don't get angry.

vii.

Once I sat on the toilet in our
railroad-style apartment in San Francisco
and composed a whole poem
instead of throwing my screaming child
against the living room wall.
The poem had a redemptive knife in it.

viii.

Satanism is just
one flip of a coin
from the church.
I was Catholic.
I was a nun.
What a gamble.

Well, that is dishonest.
The Catholic rite is sanitized,
the blood is well disguised as wine,
the flesh as bread.
There are no baby bodies, only Christ's.
For years we did not chew the host.

On the other hand, the Baltimore Catechism was
quite clear. This was the body. This was the blood.
And later we did chew as I recall. Chewed and smiled.

This was not sinister.

ix.

I believe those studies,
how many of us would pull the switch on a stranger.
Electrocution on command.

x.

Do you notice something here?
It is easier to head for third base
where the victimizer is
than run to first
where victims are
if fate drops you on a neutral second base
(where no one stays).
The game calls for clockwise rotation.
There is no chalk line straight home
and the crowd would boo.

xi.

Giles said to his wife first and then to me:
you Catholics know nothing of evil.
That was last year.
This year Gail said the same thing to Zarod and me.
Is it common knowledge?
Has everyone but me known this all along?

xii.

I have a twisted wish to get to thirteen.
See? I am not immune.

xiii.

Having arrived,
I find the number
neither cursed
nor evil
but only this—
an entity inside a universe
as wide as one and three.

Scavenger Hunt

O my many,
hardly any.

Be nice,
be nice.

Here comes a basket of bitters.
Yum yum.
(We had wanted something much larger.
O brightness.
O chewy complexity)

Hush now,
they won't know
what you're
talking about

And why not?

Whose voice should they decide this is?

It's cunningly plural.
They will think this is the client
speaking her piece.
Ho ho.

Look here,
we just must
say something
that's clear.

Hey hey.

All right, you said.
Let them, you said,

those shy selves
coming out
from under
umbrella—

Had permission, yes yes.
I see your distress.

And your problem is?

I thought they'd be young,
at least some,
and more fun,
like a picnic
in springtime,
all sunny,
yum yum.

You have longed for
a basket of bitters
and therefore
made it up.
Will you speak
one word of truth?

Can't, can't, can't.
Cant
cant
cant.

Can can.
So dance my sweet darling.

I shan't.

How many voices does it take
to make a poem?

More than two I'll tell you that.
Two is talking through your hat.

Sweet couplet
and true at last.

And so she proceeded,
spinning thin things
around an absent center.

Well, hardly. Try again.

And so she proceeded,
spinning the thin thread thing
round and round and round and round
a mystery center of sound—

in terror it all would unwind
just behind.

Well then, wobbly,
uncushioned,
the sweet little center would sit,
biting her black fingernails.
Crunch crunch.

I like a good crunch for my lunch!

I'm happy for you.
Nevertheless,
here we are
just we two
voices now.

And so
we find
the binary bind.
Where are the others?

Here others,
here others,
kitty kitty kitty kitty.

One other sits
crunching her nails,
I suppose.
Is it time?

It is time.
Sweet Honey of the Delicious Nails,
will you speak to us?

      I am much too young
      to speak to such as you

And ancient too,
we think.

      Ah ancient, yes,
      methinks.

What diction!
Is this fiction or —
are you a poet?

      Only in play

You don't say.
And when do you play?

      Between bites.

What have you to say?

      Set your sights.

And there's the blasted hook.

We don't know where to look.

    It helps,
    I've found,
    to look
    around.

Is that in a circle
or out to the sky?

    Take your pick and tell me why

What if my pick
is less sharp
than your quick,
cute reply?

    You're stalling.
    Your engine's run down.
    You want more from me
    than a smile or a frown.
    You forget that you just made me up.

I hear a bell.
Oh it's clanging and calling.
It must be time to sup.

We'll eat more than nails.
We'll dine on snails
and puppy dog tails.

Along with sugar and spice.

Be nice! Be nice!
Eat your food with sugar 'n' spice!

    O my many,
    hardly any.

Dialogue

I said to her:
Breaking through is like
breaking open an egg—
better have a bowl ready.

She said to me, somewhat later:
I would have preferred hard-boiled.
What are we / doing with / scrambled?

**At the Play Table
with the 6-yr-old Personality
of the 32-yr-old Woman**

—I ain't scared.
—Oh, me neither, Sweetie.
—Let's be not scared together, OK?

Which didn't happen. For one thing I
wouldn't call her Sweetie and for
another if I joined the denial this way I
wouldn't publish it. As for line three
it's pure wish fulfillment.

I must be lonely
sitting here with her.

Hard Day at Work

i.

I might throw up more than she wants—apronfuls of
It Could Be This / It Could Be That
sharply flapped.

Remember how we used do that,
put stones in our aprons,
see who could flap hardest,
get highest? I could try that today,
make rain from my Big Mama Apron—
because she says You Never SAY Anything.
Pronouncements, suggestions,
words thicker than gravity the
cloud of them gets large and
dark put your blond head back
and open your sweet thirsty mouth.
Swallow what falls from the sky.

How they emptied,
those aprons!

ii.

I do talk. I'm not one of those
silent therapists, legs crossed,
hands folded, Watching.
But, hell, I don't know what—
She's right. I haven't said anything
useful to her for
three weeks.

I'm *thinking*. If she could
turn me inside out,

flap ME empty,
she'd be surprised how many—
jewels, some of them,
but uncut; or maybe just
beach stones. I can't get my
fingers on them either.
Reach into my brain,
what action, all those folds,
constant vibration—
there's plenty that's hers;
nuggets and nuggets.
But nothing ready.
Nothing hauled up front.

iii.

Now look what we've done.
One more time into the illusion,
she and I headlong together,
that my words—

iv.

Maybe she's lonely
sitting here with me.

Miriam Talks a Lot, and Fast

Miriam hangs onto language.
A foolish pendulation—
high heels kicking chaos,
the elements as inchoate as
floating little mild green translucent
near-shapes.

Miriam's language is her
trapeze bar. She
swings from it,
swings from it,
swings from it.

Beyond Reverie

Yesterday in reverie
responsibility
was protean:

a spray in the brain,
a moral abstraction,
a fine sifted mist in the mind;

or a multi-colored tangle of liquid thread,
fragile, difficult to sort out;

or the thread was not liquid;
thickening, it became tough string
and knotted itself,
but in the wrong places.

I wanted more bulk, and something still
to contemplate.
But if responsibility was a sculpture,
it was a moving sculpture,
with slippery and interchangeable parts.
One blink, and the gestalt shifted.
This was a thing not amenable
to further solidification.

Today Justine is planning
to kill herself. She does not know
she is planning to kill herself,
not in her usual mind.
But she has other minds
with access to guns.

I want her to come here, stand planted,
face the impossible block,

feel for a handle to hold,
grasp it, or ask me for help.

But she has sly minds
with quick fingers to cover her eyes
and a past filled with crueler blindfolds.

I am left sighted and frightened.
Responsibility becomes a lump
and solider than what I wanted yesterday.

Alien

She is not resigned to her existence,
feels flung into her here by cruel god
who laughs the laugh that echoes off
the hollow of her hurting head;
head set off separate on the god's pet rock,
as Dali might have done, but daily;
not of night this wild displacement
being not in dream
but common as oatmeal for breakfast
if she could eat which on some days
to her distress she can.
That head is neatly placed, quite firmly
centered on the gray-green god-size rock—
rock pure, free from the other green
and even the other gray
of something living clinging,
no brave blade cutting up to air,
no lichen even; nothing such;
a simple, clear, and dry sterility.
This is a rock of god, not made by nature.
The rest of her is planted in a garden
but the garden is inside the mirror world.
Fertility is focused on the worm whose
appetite is wonderful and will eat her.

I sit inside the luck of being I have felt
and wonder what to do. My mind is hiding
in the big pants pocket of an overall I wore
around the time of psychedelia. Once on acid
my mirrored face split into segments—
green pieces set off by the lines a finger makes
with finger paint in kindergarten or
when young adults decide to play with art
while making love, not war.
A face all segmented like that in green

could easily get set inside the mirror world
of her who is forever unresigned to being.
A face like that could know the overlarge and
hungry worm. But I did not indulge in acid much
beyond that mirror time, as I recall.

And she does not indulge in images as ugly as
a large pet rock of god. She merely wishes not to be.
The sterile rock and deadly garden come from me.

Overdose

Insomniac again, I give in, open my
incorrigible eyes, and am struck:
half moon through the new skylight—
bright rind, a duller pulp,
the whole phenomenon
too white to eat and more like
sculpture anyway; cosmic crafting,
plenty of glow, classic emanation
from the inedible rind.

                I shall call it
Josephine's moon after the second
anniversary. Two years dead and
then what? Do you glow yet, Jo?
Are you edible? What is your
half-life? Dare I touch you?

And I wonder where the dark part is.

Peek-a-boo in the black night,
Jodie of you grinning the grin,
splashing in puddles,
finally crying.
Then, damn you,
dying.

Grief

Lives in the old time—
when the bill collector came to the house—
you never knew when—
or what door—

Turns

Great Lizards displaced.
Komodo dragon—
Chameleon—
Suddenly shrunken,
scurry under rock.
Ear openings,
moveable eyelids—
wait for the Big Bright Sun.

This side still dark.
The trick is in staying.
The flat earth still turns.
For the duration you can count on it.

Very little grows tall here.
There is a broad flat horizon.
At noon you can see a long way.

Even the held breath
  finally curves
    back on itself
      inside the community of breathers
        —bold circle.

Hard Drawn

Dark strokes
Hard drawn
Pencil black
Soft lead
Number two
Bea drew.

Roughly vertical
Each stroke
Whole hand
Pulled down
Time/space
Fully drawn.

Both dimensions thickening
old duplicities prepare to spring
through strong strokes
of hard drawn
roughly vertical
black lines.

Running away, skinny and young
Home town back woods
With roughly large and vertical men
In frantic motion after her
The nearly invisible next self
Hiding behind a pencil stroke.

Found her.

Monologue with Brief Chorus

January

You were right about the crowded theater
and someone yelling fire. The exit
is no good if jammed. We got confused.
We thought you meant it when you
made your invitation. Come on out,
you said. Safe to tell now,
you said. Use words.
As if you dangled liberation
for the damned. The press against hell's door
would be like this. A hiss upon
the fire of the mind, and you the one
stood up and yelled. And we the fools.
And still we search for words.

February

And find just one.
Here's *chaos* on a silver platter.
Have it as an appetizer, finger food.
The cook has fainted on the floor.
Long time before there will be more.
Eat hearty.

April

Today I think of language as blocks.
I pick them up, position them;
make and make and make a thing.
I cannot be more thoughtfully specific,
even, dear therapist, for you. Not yet.

77

June

These blocks are not as blank
as you might be imagining.
Each side contains a flattened scene
done like a queen on a playing card,
and (can you understand?) alive.
The flatness and aliveness coincide,
a trembling, gesturing sculpture
done in low relief. Circumstances
make the building vulnerable.
My least ambitious towers tend to fall.

November

The cook has served us up some soup.
Do you really want to eat with me?
This table and these chairs
are made from living blocks
which only intermittently consent
to function as furniture.
You are welcome to sit for the moment.
Do you really want to eat with me?

The good thing about soup is the mystery.
You remain in the dark
about what you consume
and it's cooked well enough to digest.

This is a new recipe, my own alphabet.
Do you really want to eat with me?

January

After dinner, theater.
Someone sweep the sawdust, please.

Get that lady a folding chair.
First you eat, then you see.
Here in the round, fire confined,
exits multiple, enter the mind.

See the dancing shadow bear,
see the puppet climb the air.
Here is a circus with sirens for song.
Sing along.

This production is the result of many
months of community labor. Funding
has come from anonymous sources
dedicated to the proposition that
the play's the thing in which they'll catch
the conscience. Ballots will be provided
for final judgment. Audience by
invitation only. Welcome.

Act One. Birth trauma by
forceps month six. Doctors with
dirty hands and assorted other parts.

Act Two. The usual. Incest by night. School by day.

Act Three. Long packed summer dirt with
large rocks. Cold moon by flame.
(X-rated segments of play. Blindfolds provided.)

Epilogue. Escape through locked door
by means of safecracking skills
acquired at uncle's knee age three.

See the dancing shadow bear,
see the puppet climb the air.
Here is a circus with sirens for song.
Sing along.

<u>April:</u>

After the play, something changed.
We know, but we can't feel.
Shuffle the cards.

<u>July:</u>

              We merge and separate
on the same day. I feel a holy confusion.
Come with me to the door of the theater,
my own mind. I will speak to you
about the things inside. I will
shake but manage. Later,
I will turn and look at you.

Epilogue

In Gratitude

*(The seasoned therapist
speaks to her clients.)*

That green surprise of passion, wild with red
and glowing holy, now has seen the coming
and the going of the years. The tender verdancy
of spring; high hot sun of summer; the drama
of the dying fall; stark winter, white and gray:
have all grown common. I love the common,
like a rock worn smooth by tides that come and go.

You are to me like rocks, a substance in my life;
part, now, of my foundation. I am built on you
and other things. Today I like the house I am,
the weathering of me.

Shirley Glubka was born in Washington, D.C. in 1942. She grew up in Minnesota and now lives in Maine.

She holds a Masters Degree in Psychology from The Fielding Institute and a Masters Degree in English from the University of Maine. She has a private practice as a Clinical Counselor.

A member of the International Society for the Study of Dissociation, she was co-founder, with Virginia Holmes, Ph.D and Carol Romeo Veits, L.C.S.W., of the Bangor Area Forum for the Study of Multiple Personality and Dissociation.

Shirley has had prose and poetry published in a variety of places, including *Many Voices: Words of Hope for People Recovering from Trauma and Dissociation; Lesbians at Midlife: The Creative Transition; Conditions; Sinister Wisdom; Feminist Studies; Mothers Who Leave: behind the myth of women without their children; All American Women; Women in American Culture; Sun Dog; Tinker's Shop; Potato Eyes; Kennebec: Portfolio of Maine Writing; Technology of the Sun; Out of the Cradle: an Uncommon Reader; Seems; naming: poems by 8 women;* and *WomanSpirit.*

Green Surprise of Passion is her first book.

To order send $12 check or money order
(includes shipping & handling)
with your name & address to:

Blade of Grass Press
R.F.D. 1, Box 1358
Stockton Springs, Maine 04981